I0172794

Minds

@

Work

2

An Anthology Of Poems

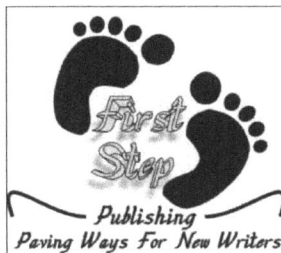

First
Step

Publishing
Paving Ways For New Writers

First Published in India in 2014 by First Step Publishing

Editorial / Sales / Marketing Office at
303-304 Garnet Nirmal Lifestyles Ph 2
Behind Nirmal Lifestyles Mall
LBS Marg Mulund West
Mumbai 400080
E-Mail:- info@firststepcorp.com
www.firststepcorp.com

ISBN: - 978-93-83306-06-0
Publisher and Managing Editor: Rohit Shetty
Cover Designed by: Design Fishing
Managing Design Editor: Rohit Shetty
Editing: Rohit Shetty
Typeset in Book Antique
Price: ₹ 180 Paperback
Available as an Android App on Playstore

Rohit Shetty

Indian Literary Industry has come up with many authors who have received both national and international acclaim but amidst this, poetry has been sidelined and publishers do not publish poetry stating the lack of market, and as a result many talented writers or I must say poets fail to get their books out or get their poems published. First Step Publishing realises this situation and has come up with a collection of poems from poets across India, poets coming from all walks of life, Doctors, Engineers, Bankers, Students, Homemakers, Previously published poets, many to be published for the first time.

Minds@Work is an annual book by First Step Publishing. Minds@Work 2 had no topic or content to be printed till I had a casual discussion with one of the entrants over coffee and realised that an anthology of poems can be done for this edition, so an online campaign was started calling in for entries. We were overwhelmed with the kind of response we received and had a tough time in selecting poets as every entry deserves to be a part of Minds@Work2.

I would like to thank the entire team of First Step Publishing for making a casual talk a working reality and also Design Fishing for the beautiful cover and our associates, Speak Out Newspaper for Branding and Promotions and First Step Corp for designing and developing our Android App.

In the end my love and warm regards to all the readers.

Contents

Shalini Katyal

Born and brought up in Delhi, Shalini is pursuing her Masters in English from IGNOU and also learning French since the past year and a half.

Shalini sees beauty from all walks of life and seeks inspiration from all of God's creations.

She has a deep inclination towards philosophy and poetry. An avid reader, she loves absorbing romance which also happens to be her favourite genre apart from pondering over philosophy. Apart from being an avid reader she is also a part anthologies like *Uff Yeh Emotions 2* by General Press, and *U me and Zindagi* by Omji Publication Being a lover of music, she believes that there is nothing like a good song to impress her. She can be reached at shel.katyal5577@gmail.com.

Shalini Katyal

Silent Departure

You left me by gifting tears to my eyes; pain to my
heart,
Your silent departure my love tearing me apart!

I keep on contemplating what could be the possible
reasons,
I keep on blaming and isolating myself season after
season,
I keep trying to figure out why you took that
unexpected decision!

If only I knew one day you would leave me without
saying a word,
I would have embraced you tight, sealed you in my
own world!

Past memories are the only thing left to me,
The touch of your lips is just so fresh on me.
The love talks which you used to whisper in my ears,
Those soothing tunes of romance are killing me by
oozing tears.

Come back to me, I still await you,
Don't leave me to die when you are not there to
rescue
My heart is refusing to except your sudden and silent
adieu!"

Melting Desires

"Feeling loved by lying under the shady moon's
cocoon,
Night is glowing astoundingly in the month of the
monsoon.
Dampness soothing the core of her heart,
For light rain keeps on leaving its enduring mark!

Night is flaunting its beauty tingling with fragility,
She is kissing the moon with deep dependability!

Soaked completely in the sea of sensuous feelings,
She is experiencing a different course of healing!

Night is all set to merge into sparkling moonlight,
Love birds singing songs of amour by seeing this
mesmerizing sight.
Stars wrapping themselves up in the covering of
clouds, feeling shy and stretching wide,
For this is a private moment: 'a moment of sheer
pride'!

The night is no more silent now; moon is there to give
her words,
To pull her out of her gloominess,
To accompany her always in this lonely world! "

Shalini Katyal

<u>Canvas Of Life</u>

"On the canvas of life, we sketch dreams and desires,
Make them colourful with the brush of flaming inner
fires.
Some appreciate the art making it seem higher,
Some make fun, by passing a laugh of satire!

Some throw unappealing colours, bent on destroying
its beauty,
Frustrations and failures are the pushing force behind
this atrocity.
Remember always, only one canvas is gifted to each
soul and entity,
To beautify it whole life, is your moral duty!

God has blessed us with the options of choosing
colours,
Despite this, some fools go for black and grey covers.
People fail to grab the shades which the rainbow
showers,
Disrespecting the nature, by ignoring all its favours!

Walk proudly by holding canvas on each life's path,
Sprinkle shades of faith with determined heart!"

A Note Of Thanks

"Whenever I close my eyes, I see your loving
reflection,
Looking intensely into my eyes, depicting an image of
perfection.
You have always expressed your love without the
tinge of deception,
Whole life I'll be thanking you, holding in heart deep
admiring affection!

You have never left me in the fragile moments of our
association,
We fought; we cried but never dipped into the sea of
separation.
After every fight you held me in your arms with
tender emotions,
Whole life I'll be cherishing such remarkable
connections!

Once, when we were walking near the seashore,
You held me tight, pulled me closer.
Placed your lips over mine, wrapped my tongue in
protective enclosure,
Whole life I'll be kissing these moments with such
sensational pleasures!

My eyes are wet by embracing tremendous
sentiments,

Only you are the reason behind its sparkling
contentment's.
The guardians of true love protects us from being
distance
Whole life I'll be supporting you, walking beside your
existence!"

A Mirror Of Life

"Each person's life has a journey of its own.
Some walk on the carpet of roses,
Some endure the wrath of thorns!

Some kiss the beauty of their good fortune,
Some embrace a blemished misfortune.
Life keeps on moving on the biased wheel of fortune!

Life is a book of unpredictable occurrences.
The thickness of which depends on God's
preferences,
A few chapters remain blank to be filled with new
acquaintances!

Memories are the mirror of a bygone time that the
candle of past will lit.
Captured images of remorse could be seen in it,
Blissful moments could be replayed in it!

Holding the hand of life, time is running fast,
Before it gets too late, complete your each assigned
task.
Life is too short to be soaked into regretful sobbing
past!"

<u>Sandhita Agarwal</u>

She is a quiet ambivert who enjoys long walks in the woods alone and admiring nature. When not watching a horror movie she loves spending her time studying the human behavior and its delicate intricacies. You can reach her at evening_sun2000@yahoo.com

The Race..

I've my running shoes on
I can hear the siren call
My elbows are protected
Lest I should fall

I feel the wind in my face
The concrete beneath my feet
The music in my ears
Run run run run

Compatriots run behind and ahead
Run run run run
My mind is numb
Run run run run

My legs feel tired
The soles grow tattered
But I still run run
run run run run

And then without a warning
There are tears in my eyes
I can't blink them away
I've got to run run run run

the pain hits me in the chest
but its not a heart attack

Sandhita Agarwal

It's just my heart being sad
I am stopping I can't run run run run

I've stopped.
I am sitting in the middle of the path
With my head in my hands
Compatriots run run run run

They smile as they look at me
Pity, jealousy, arrogance, defiance??
I start screaming in my head
I am not able to run run run run

I am all alone
I am the only one still
The terror is alive
I am doing what I was always afraid of
I am not running

I can't open my eyes
What will I find?
Are the stories true
I am not able to run run run run

Aeons are passing by
I am not able to open my eyes
I am not able to run run run run
I am not able to run run run run

I can't keep my eyes closed anymore
I am getting hurt on the road
I look around and see
Trees birds and bees

The fear is slowly leaving me
This is nothing like the stories
I strut my way along
Looking at the things around me

I look look look look
The trees the sky the birds and the bees
The leaves the grass the squirrels
And I can't stop looking

But then I look at my compatriots
And then I think run run
But I don't give in to the call
And I only look look look look

How there's beauty in me
Look look look look
How fun it is just to BE
Look look look look

Sandhita Agarwal

<u>Trying to find myself again</u>

How lonely I feel
In the darkness where I kneel
I'm trying to find
The one I left behind

The pain is so real
The wounds can't seem to heal
When did I lose you
What can I do

Have I lost you forever
Can we never be togther
I am sorry I said before
But you don't listen to me anymore

How lonely I feel
Life has lost all its appeal
Oh my earth show me the way
In the darkness here I pray

The Dark Passenger

I gave you air to breathe
I gave you eyes to see
I gave you wings to fly
I gave you my belief

I only wanted strength from you
I wanted to hide forever
From this world without virtue
But what did you do?

You turned my weakness into your own strength
You pushed me into a deep dark trench
You grew stronger than me everyday
You betrayed me in every possible way

You want me frozen in time
Stuck at one place all my life
You want me to hate
All the love that I have

But know this now
I will fight you somehow
I am now strong and wise
I won't make the same mistake twice

Sandhita Agarwal

Empty

Everything that i have felt
In this lifetime of regret
Living in a shell of pain
Can I start back again

I felt happiness
I felt joy
When he was by my side
I felt happy to be alive

He was my friend
He was my companion
I was empty when he came
I am empty now he's gone

Chase away the nights
Erase those memories
Heal my tainted wounds
Can I turn back time?

I don't want love
I don't want fame
I just want to heal
And be whole someday

This void inside of me
Is killing me everyday

This darkness inside
That no light can pierce

I must continue on my journey
To discover the truth
The truth will save me
The truth alone will heal me.

Sandhita Agarwal

The Demons

I stand here in front of the mirror
An empty glare, no reflection
I ask myself when it happened
The silence a vacuous rejection

Every word left unsaid
Every missing link
Every tear left unshed
I regret everything

You tried to help
Tried to set me free
But the demons were stronger
We were never meant to be

I have become a slave
A puppet to their whims
Every day an unwritten horror
Every night a tormented bliss

The demons have fed me
On fear n sorrow
I have nothing left in me
No hopes for tomorrow

I have to let go now
Dont ask me why
I am the demons
And this is my goodbye

Ila Garg

"Ila Garg is a girl next door, born in Jaipur, currently residing in Delhi. She has completed her graduation in English Literature and pursuing Masters in English & Communication Studies at present. She loves writing. She has a flair for words. It is a passion; a compulsion; something that gives her an avenue to express herself. She writes when she is happy; when she is angry or when an issue touches her heart. She resorts to writing when she is restless or when she is on the verge of breaking down.

Creativity and writing has always been attracting her. Apart from being an avid reader, writer, reviewer, and editor, she is an active blogger too. She blogs at www.ilashininggem.blogspot.in, where you can find some of her articles, poetry, random thoughts, interviews, movie and book reviews.

Her debut novel, titled, 'Life and Promises' is to be released on 1st Jan'14 and her next novel, titled, 'Cheer up! The worst is yet to come' is slated to be released soon after. One of her short stories is a part of an anthology, 'A Night in Paradise'.

She can be contacted at:

Email - ilagarg@ymail.com

Ila Garg

<u>As I looked within...I saw!</u>

Walking down the lane,
Viewing the street with disdain.
My mind loaded with so many heavy thoughts,
Questions are there, but answers are not.

I keep moving, dejected,
Evil happenings keep me distracted.
How can I shut my mind?
How can I keep myself denied?

You tell me, can't you see?
What's going on around us? Around me?
Forlorn, lost all happiness,
I stood there in distress.

I looked at the street,
Found it full of bloodshed.
I looked at the people at a distance,
Found them crying profusely.

I looked at the nature,
Found it all in an utter mess.
And then I looked within myself,
I was astonished with what I saw there.

I saw a girl weeping,
She had been raped.

I saw a poor man begging,
He was helpless.

I saw a crowd lying in blood,
They were the victims of a bomb blast.
I saw an innocent bride being burnt,
She was the victim of the dowry custom.

I saw a pool of blood and a knife,
A boy had committed suicide tired of the stress,
maybe.
I saw a large piece of barren land,
It was the victim of the selfish men.

In addition, I saw accidents, thievery,
And what not! I saw a lot.
And I wondered where are we living?
And my heart cringes with pain.

I feel hollow, I feel bitter,
I feel so unsafe, and I feel dead.
Lost in my oblivion world,
I try in vain to remove this evil somehow.

I shift towards my poetic delusions,
Frantically trying to find an escape route in them.
But am so hurt, so much disturbed,
That even my poetry has started reflecting my pain.

Ila Garg

It fails to calm me down,
It fails to bring a smile on my face.
I wish somehow the clock turns around,
And we go back to what we were!

Dark Colours

When in life you badly fail
And you are no longer capable to sail
You feel lonely
There is sadness only

And you run as you cry
You can no longer try
All your laughter is gone
You curse the day you were born

All your dreams are shattered
The pain no longer mattered
You are tired of fighting
And you want to go in a hiding

The failure grips you
The weakness catches you
No one to share your feelings with
No one to sit with

No one can understand you
You feel that the whole world is cursing you
All the happiness has been squeezed out
You want to just shout and shout

All your spirits dampen
Sometimes it just happens

Ila Garg

It's like a silent blast
It gives a familiar ache that lasts

You let your emotions flow
But you don't want to show
Your life turns black and white
And there is no light

You feel it is the end of the world
You want to get curled
But no sympathizing arms are around
No humble and relaxing sound

You want to moan
You want to be left alone
You don't know what to do
You just keep on feeling blue

Such sad moments leave a mark
That makes your world look so dark
These dark colors win your soul
You even forget your goal

Everyone just blames you
And they hate you
But one thing they don't know
In life, it is important to fail too...

Endless Wait

I keep turning pages as I sit in vain,
Sometimes I walk alone through the lane.
Memories haunt and they turn me restless,
And all of a sudden I feel worthless.

It happens every single time,
The same story, the same rhyme.
I am so tired of living the same dread,
It makes me go almost dead.

It's like a blackout, no hope at all,
All my words are but a drawl.
There's something missing in my life,
I guess it's happiness for which my heart thrive.

I keep waiting endlessly at a corner,
But I never hear your voice or even a whisper.
I keep waiting for the answer to my questions,
Or may be just some suggestions.

I miss you or I miss myself more,
You love me? I'm not sure.
Your absence kill me each day,
Still I wait for you and I pray.

This distance between us makes me cry,
I just want to smile now, I won't lie.

Ila Garg

This vainness is turning me insane,
The sheer loneliness lands me in immense pain.

The shadows from the past engulf me,
Resurrecting silence is not letting me flee.
Everything has turned so harsh and bone-chilling,
Am walking in your quest and struggling.

This wait is quite challenging; for me, for you,
It's like an unsolved mystery, with no clue.
Gushes of wind blowing through my hair,
Whisper your name, and reminds me of your care.

Stars in the sky accompany me, wink at me,
They assure me of a good time and make me see;
How near it is. I think I may be lost now and should
moan,
But you must know, I'm not coming back, at least not
alone.

I Lose It All...

I cry, I smile, I rise, I fall,
And then slowly, I lose it all.
I feel sadness around me,
Engulfing me, I don't feel free.

Deep down my heart is hollow,
So much sadness, that it can't swallow.
It pinches, it cringes, It is shattered now,
Though its hard, but I am surviving somehow.

Bomb blasts, blood sheds, all around,
Inglorious acts have an effect so profound.
Gunshots in the air has left no safe place,
I am sick and tired of seeing this face.

This earth has turned all filthy, rotten curse,
We are only making the conditions worse.
I fear everything, everyone, every day,
How long will we keep bearing this way?

What are we supposed to do?
Sit and wait to die? Cry? Oh no!
No more tears, no more fears.
We have to save ourselves and our dears.

Death is a natural end, it should come naturally,
Men should not bring it to us willingly.

But I just find myself helpless at the mercy of the
system,
A system that exists on papers, merely as an idiom.

I cry, I smile, I rise, I fall,
And then slowly, I lose it all.
My mind gets heavy of over thinking,
My eyes tired, sleep - deprived, without blinking.

I can feel myself falling down now,
Because its hard for me to pretend now.
There is an emptiness residing within me,
Someday soon, I hope to break free...

Pool of Blood and Pain

I sit on the edge of a pool for hours,
Pool filled with blood, pain, and misery.
Am trapped in an invisible cage,
In worries am embedded.
It's like my soul is cringing, yelling in pain.
Lifeless, is what I feel mostly.
My body is becoming hollow gradually,
I hear voices, vehemently painful voices.
Blood, blood, blood,
Is all what I see.
Pain, pain, pain,
Is all what I feel.

Silence screams at me,
That feeling of nothingness grips me.
Faint sounds of laughter strike in my ears,
But alas, I have forgotten even to smile,
Let alone laugh.
Unaccustomed pain has taken it all away.
The emptiness is closing on me now.
My life is a stand still, no joy.
Insomnia, is ruling. I can't even rest.
Yes, I am hurt, brutally hurt,
May be now am getting used to this pain.
I can't think of anything beyond this,
I am drowning in my own tears.

Ila Garg

No air to breath, no desire to live,
Only a tortured soul resides within.
Death would be better than life,
But death doesn't come easy.
The pool keeps increasing in volumes,
Now I have reached right in the middle.
I wish I could reach the other side,
Before I can cross, I am forced to give up,
To surrender to the enormous pain,
And be so weak that I am unable to walk.
I am gradually becoming dizzy,
Numb, frozen, my mind and senses blocked.
Should I keep fighting in vain?
Should I be strong and tell someone?
Should I just be a slave to this harassment?
Should I surrender to this endless torture?
Should I kill myself before this pain kills me?
I guess yes! Dying would be much better after all.
At least I will catch on some peace at last.

Barkha Parikh

Barkha Parikh is an I.T. engineer and also a Computer teacher from Ahmedabad, Gujarat. She is an avid reader.. She writes for a Cause and Not for an Applause and the cause is – "To touch many hearts and Enlighten many souls." She believes in "Live in Present because Present means a Gift." Her only mantra in life is – "I romance words, I write."

Barkha Parikh

This post is totally dedicated to "Mumbai Photo Journalist Gang rape" case.. Wish she gets justice soon.. and resumes her life back with head held high... Feeling sad and annoyed..

A Brutal Act

There she was, Happily clicking the pictures, Writing a fable..
How less she knew, that soon her confidence is going to get disable..

By lots of men, she got grabbed..
With tears of blood, her body dabbed..

The act so brutal..
The man so cruel..

The old factory proves to be the scariest memory..
The day that ended up so dreary…

Wish the victim gets the justice on time..
And the culprits are considered in society, a grime…

Hope she resumes her life soon with pride..
Peace, Happiness and Justice are showered on her with a Stride..!!

Every Time it Rains

I still remember those moments, Every time it Rains..
My Emotions become Perfect Blend of Pleasure and
Pains..
Your touch so gentle, Your hug so warm..
Your eye lashes bore the rain drops, adding the
charm..
At the road stalls, we drank the tea made of ginger…
The clanging of cups raised in cheers, of new joys to
come it was a harbinger..
The way our eyes met, taking every single sip..
The way we laughed our tears out when the biscuit
broke in the tea when u dipped..
The way you made me feel safe, Covering me with
your coat...
Paper boats on which we wrote our names, Made our
emotions float..
The way we danced in the rain, to the beat of the rain
drops..
The flowers, the breeze and our bodies were the
major props..
The tiny droplets travelling through my tresses
landing on my neck..
The tickling effect they created made me give u sweet
peck…
I try to still catch the rain drops in my palm, but they
slip out..

Barkha Parikh

Now I just get wet, The feeling is lost that once
flipped out..
I know you cry sitting up above, adding Your Tears
to the Rain...
I still remember those moments, Every time it Rains..!!

Just keep my Words Alive

Time is slipping away, in a stride, out of my Hand...
Out of the fist, Just as the Summer Sand,

The scribbling that I write in my crisp white virgin
pages may turn tomorrow to yellow...
The deepest of my feelings and the emotions I put in,
may feel tomorrow shallow...

My laughter aloud, my endless blabber, my
mischievous wink,
Someday, it may all be gone just in a blink...

The words I pen down, as pearls on the paper that are
neatly beaded...
May break the string, off to the floor may be
headed...

Don't lose hope, I still always shall be around and
near...
To bring a smile on everyone's face, who have been to
me quite dear...

My hugs, my kisses, my cares, my love...
I shall always be showering from up above...

The fact today may become tomorrow A Fantasy...
My Words are my Only Legacy...

Barkha Parikh

I may not be around, but don't let me fade in your remembrances…
It's a request, Just keep my Words Alive as my reminiscences…!

This poem is dedicated to my mentor- Barkha Parikh

Thank You

"I still Memorize Every Word you Spoke
The flow of your teachings with which my mind
soaked..

I may not be a perfect disciple of your worth
That's d reason hesitate at times to come forth

I always have looked at you with gleaming eyes
Admiring every step of yours and trying to be
likewise

The way You used to step in the school spreading
your fragrance with the morning breeze
No matter how many worries and tensions I had, it
always brought me to ease..

The way You carried Ur Beauty and Grace...
You always looked Dignified with an Angel Face...

Your eyes like the sparkling stars that shine bright...
When everything around is dark, it gave light...

The way you tilt your head when you laugh...
And that always makes raise my career graph

Barkha Parikh

The way you give a witty comment with an innocent
smile
All my tears and worry bees fly away in a while

You have always taught me how to Live n Forgive
And have taught me Love n Cares is all I must Give…

Time may pass and get coiled into a reel…
But no one can ever abolish how special u made me
feel…

You taught me lots of things…
And thereby gave birth to my wings…

You have been a candle spreading your Light…
The wings that you gave me have made me reach this
height…

You came to my Life and Turned it Right Around…
I am always happy now and Never feel down…

You have always whispered your thoughts n teaching
sweetly into my ears…
Since that I have smiled forever without any fear…

When the Things were too tough for me to handle…
You have proved yourself to be for me a God's
Angel…

You may not Sprinkle on me the Magic Fairy Dust…
But you have always guided me what is to be done
Must..

May God Listen to your words and hear your every
need…
I too will be praying for you, asking God to first grant
your wishes indeed…

Wherever you have walked you have left a trace
I have yearned to have what you have – 'GRACE'

I am short of words to explain how I Feel…
All I can do is, Join My Hands and Kneel…

I worship you for being what You are…
And I celebrate You for being what You are…

My Life, I owe to You, is because all that u have
inspired
To stay in Ur Memories is all I have desired…

For You, I am always going to be there
And give u huge amounts of LOVE n CARE"

Barkha Parikh

Truly, Madly, Deeply Chocoholic

The darkest secret that tempts me to savour,
The rich bitter cocoa bean mingled in you and its
flavor,

A temptation that can't be avoided by masses…
Just as the spell enchanted by some enchantress…

Just like a kid, I see chocolate mountains and rivers in
my fantasy…
And every bite of your smooth brown beauty revives
my ecstasy…

The way you melt in my mouth, makes my heart melt
for you…
Grand seductress is what my sweet tooth felt for
you…

The way when u r combined with rum and raisins…
To get you and have you, I am all ready to be a part of
your any sin…

You are a friend in pleasure, a healer in pain…
In your presence, everything else seems disdain…

A little bit of orange and hazelnut blends with you
well…

I might have to re-incarnate to break that casted
spell…

The blood in the body of others may be Red as the
nose of Clown…
But by mingling with you, I doubt my blood has also
turned Darkest Brown…

No matter how much My Life has been Melancholic…
But I am dedicated to you loyally, Being Truly,
Madly, Deeply Chocoholic…!!

Sanhita Baruah

Recognized for her contribution in "Uff Ye Emotions", an anthology of love stories, and "Kaleidoscope", a multi-genre anthology, Sanhita Baruah, born in the beautiful and diverse state of Assam, is a Software Engineer by profession. She also runs a blog titled "Pens and Pages" at http://sanhitabaruah9.blogspot.in/ and many of her articles and poems have been published in National and International Journals and Magazines

Embracing The Winter You Left

Let that summer be yours
and this winter, it will be mine to keep...

the ever expanding white
and the naked tree standing alone shamelessly
let the green that once was, be yours
and this pallidity will be mine to keep...

the coldness the sun fails to obliterate
the darkness that falls sooner than ever
let that warmth bygone be yours
this solitude will be mine to keep...

Lost...

If only tears could heal
If only ruminating could cure
You would have been hale by now
Because I cried for you
Because I thought of you

If only prayers could mend
If only intonations could restore
You would have been alive today
Because I chanted your name
Because I prayed for you

And the tears that flowed
The prayers chanted
Could do nothing
But watch silently
The act of pallid Mors
While I wept for you

And I wept for hours
Sitting beside your cold cadaver
Hollering to waken you
Awaiting your response
With love, I kept stroking you

If only time could heal

If only memories could fade
I would have buried your thoughts by now
But ages have passed
I still remember you

And today, to my grave,
With me, I take you. . .

Sanhita Baruah

Love Perseverant

His silence was depressing
His emotions, hidden
He couldn't fake a smile anymore

Her silence was her answer
her integrity, overt
She embraced his sorrow henceforth

He walked a million miles away
she followed his steps
till the end of the day

her tears were her love
his hatred, her strength
she bore the adversities, yet walked forth

his heart did melt
in oblivion, his misery was
he couldn't evade her love anymore

His silence was warm
his emotions, at peace
he took to mend the heart he once tore

her perseverance was answered
their love bloomed
and they didn't need words anymore...

Unrequited

I thought it was love
I was sure you felt it too
and somehow I knew
for eternity I was meant for you

Dreams of you and me
with angels, in heaven
Yes, we were together
in my heart's haven

but what did happen
that every dream shattered
into pieces, they were
and my heart, utterly battered

Oh, you never loved me
and so I was left, dejected
with a painful heart
and my love, unrequited...

Dr Rajdeep Kosode

"Dr Rajdeep Kosode started writing since when he was 6. Writing poetry has always been his passion, though recently he has shifted his focus on prose. One of his short stories has been long-listed at a national level short story competition. He loves exploring most storytelling art forms, especially world-movies and graphic novels. He is a medical doctor, currently pursuing his post-graduation in Pharmacology research at New York. His interests include movies, travel and adventure sports. He is currently working on a fantasy series of his own."

Goldfish

Where do you intend to go,
O my dear goldfish?
Trapped in the nothingness,
In those blue silences.
Running after reflections
Of yourself, incessantly,
And not knowing the mirage
Is all there is to it.
Confined in a coffin,
Scratching your name
On the inside with fins,
That nobody will ever read.
And still dreaming of
The sea and the silver streams
Where you never did go
And never will....

Dr. Rajdeep Kosode

The Warrior

She reached him,
To the far end of the field.
He lay as a ball of flesh,
That was all what remained.

She now remembered him
As the father to her sons,
As a warrior above all,
And a husband to love.

Not as a helpless man,
Tied to a totem pole,
Burning from head to toe,
Melting drop by drop.

She didn't shed a tear then,
For the enemy wanted them
To cascade on from her eyes
To her cheekbones.

Now she hugged the ball
And let out a tear unwittingly
That rested on his dead flesh
And so they met for the last time.

The Fall

I slither towards darkness,
Like a monk, towards a mountain.
I move within,
As I move without;
Slowly I ascend,
The heights of darkness.

Then I stand at the peak,
And laugh at the stupidity below;
For this moment, I await
The pain of the fall.

And then I leap,
Unfettered into the light,
Into a million Suns,
Blinding me to death.

What a way to shine,
Oh; what a way to shine!

Dr. Rajdeep Kosode

Wristcutter

Slowly and steadily,

The warmth leaves my body,
Leaving me elated & cold,
As I feel the rhapsody.

The treacherous hand sniggers,
As the other sheds tears,
Tears that drain its pain,
And free it of the fears.

Swimming in the clouds,
I feel liberated again.
As if the sky is a womb,
And I am unborn again.

As I swim above, alone,
Dejected, I think of you.
Though I lament the gloom,
My grouses are still few.

For I celebrate the sorrow,
In its most primal state;
However much a heart wails,
It has to start with a new slate.

Woken out of my doze,
Piercing needles I feel,
Time to be alive again,
Haven't yet crossed the hill.

Too much joy to lose once,
Death is the absolute fun.
As the twilight judges,
Life is the one half-done.

I lay half awake in bed,
Another cut in my dreams,
Tears well up my eyes,
Nothing is what it seems....

Dr. Rajdeep Kosode

Love Story

The barren lands,
Dreamt of pregnant winds,
Even in the scorching heat.
And there were no showers,
For an intolerable eternity.
A stalking gaze then came along,
Calming the uncertainty,
Killing the fears,
And dousing the rage Of a wasteful redemption,
And saved my mirth,
From dying a thousand deaths,
Ever again,
Ever again...

Neelam Saxena Chandra

Neelam Saxena Chandra is an engineer by profession (working in Indian Railways as Director (IT)). Writing poetry and fiction is her passion. More than four hundred of her stories/poems have been published in various leading Indian magazines such as Woman's Era, Alive, Sarita, Grihshobha, Grihlaxmi, Naya Gyanodaya, Kathakram, Vanita, Nandan, Champak, Chandamama, Reader's Forum, Suman Saurabh etc as well as international journals such as Torrid Literary journal, The Camel Saloon, Inspiration magazine,

Ruminations journal, Tongue Journal, The Criterion, E-fiction, Enchanting Verses, Frog croon, Saraba, Ewoman etc. Four of her children's story books have also been published by Room to Read, Naman, Sadhna and Sahni Publications. One novel has been published by LiFi Publications and one by PAGETURN PUBLISHERS. Two Poetry books have been published - HUES OF LOVE by Writers Empire and SILHOUETTES OF REFLECTIONS by YS Books International . Ten more books are under publication including one novel by LIFI Publications, One novel by Authorspress, One short story collection in English by LiFi, Four Picture books by Rajkamal Publications, one poetry collection by AUTHORSPRESS and one short story collection in Hindi and one in English by by Omji Publishers .. Her poems/stories have been published in various international anthologies such as ON THE BRINK (By Spectacle Publishing), HEALING WAVES (By Skywarrior Publications), PHO FOR LIFE, SAARC ANTHOLOGY OF POETRY 2011, VAANI, Chicken soup , Anthology by British Council on Rabindranath Tagore, In your own words and In Priase-In memory-In Ink (Brian Wixon anthologies) etc . She has won second prize in a competition organized by Pratham Books (Chuskit competition). One of her story has won an award in a contest organized by Children Book Trust, India in 2009. She has also been awarded second prize by Gulzarji in a Poetry Contest organized by American

Society on the topic 'Poetry for Social Change'. Her book TALES FROM SUNDERVAN has been listed in the long list in children's category in the ECONOMIST CROSSWORD BOOK AWARD. The book SUNDERVAN KI KAHANIYAN has been awarded Premchand Puraskar by Ministry of Railways (II prize).

Neelam also debuted as a lyricist in Shankar Tucker's composition MERE SAJAN SUN SUN at the link http://www.youtube.com/watch?v=auRmXTmVwr Y and the song has won the POPULAR CHOICE AWARD in Folk Fusion category. in RADIO CITY FREEDOM AWARD

And Yet

Erase
All alphabets
In the book of love.

Burn
All photographs
In the album of fondness.

Trample
All traces
In the sands of time.

Extinguish
All flames
In the reign of affection.

And yet
The love shall come
Calling by.

Blossom

The heat was atrocious
The atmosphere sickening
But, I still bloomed...

Entirety seemed hostile
The paths were unwelcoming
But I still bloomed...

The soil was parched
The leaves were gasping
But I still bloomed...

I bloomed because
All the voids and empty spaces
In my life
Had been filled up
With your soothing fragrance-
Fragrance of love...

Love

Love
Is like an earthquake.

It can never be predicted
and comes suddenly
Without any warning.
It sends tremors
In the whole body.
It causes displacement
of mind and thoughts.
If the scale is large
There can be a Tsunami.
If feelings become violent
There can be volcanoes and blasts.

And the after effects-
The impacts remain embedded for long....

Much Beyond That...

Petty pleasures of life
A big bank balance
Gold and platinum jewelry
Large bungalows
Life is much beyond that...

Bodily love
Kisses and cuddling
Union of bodies
Life is much beyond that...

Oh Lord! Let me lead a life
Which embraces everything
Much beyond that...

And gifts me a love
Much beyond that...

Neelam Saxena Chandra

My Dear Pup

As I walked down the lane,
I saw a pup wriggling with hunger and pain.
Intuitively, I took it in my arms-
My caress made him cosy and warm!

In his eyes I could see a few drops of tears,
His body was a bundle of fears.
I cuddled it and fed it bread and milk
And lovingly stroked and patted his fur of silk!

Was I mistaken or had I seen a smile on his face?
As he licked my feet, I stood there amazed!
He must have been as lonely as me
For in my company he was dancing in glee!!

Now he follows me wherever I walk
And nods as if he understands all my talks
In my dear pup, I have found my best friend ever
I know our companionship shall last forever!!!

Nikhil Chandwani

Nikhil Chandwani is a published poet, author and a script writer. He is currently working for Mystic Wanderer Production House as a lead script writer for international travel show and Hollywood Movies. He has bagged
1. United Kingdom Forum Award for excellence in poetry (One of the biggest award in poetry)
2. Tamil Nadu State Award.
3. Om Press Award
The show Nikhil is writing will be telecasted on Discovery Channel from Jan 2015 onwards.

Nikhil Chandwani

His Published work includes

1) Two poetry books: Ink'd With Love and Unsung Words

2) Fiction: I wrote your name in the sky

3) Script Writer, Mystic Wanderer Production House/Discovery Channel (present)

4) Director/Story Writer at UCN News Channel. (2012-2013)

5) Presently publishing Unsung Words, the official biography of Major Dhyan Chand narrated by 1975 Worldcup winning Hockey legends.

6) Ex Chief Editor at Penumbra Magazine.

7) Guest Columnist at Lokmat Times and Stimulus India Magazine.

8) Guest Fiction Writer at Underground Voices magazine and E-Fiction India.

9) Anthologies: Taj Mahal Review

Along The Busy Road

Along the busy road,
I feel those soul so crystal blue
Your hair it falls onto your shoulders,
beauty oh so true

You glitter as you leisurely walk on by,
flawless your style
As if you "hung the moon" tonight,
You sparkle as you smile

Dressed in jeans which grasp you close,
and kindly hug your hips
Your dignified smile gives a vigorous glow,
between your humid lips

Your smell lingers in my brain,
as if to seize a pause
Fragrance assorted with your desires,
certainly is the cause

As you go by me by once more,
it calmly brushes back my hair
The odor of an angel,
to which there's no compare

You feel of prettiness and of life,
your sensation shines clean gold

Dulling all who assemble around,
a jewel to behold

As I advance you to position and welcome,
your tone rolls soft and clean
Reminding me of reassuring waters,
as they bathe on down a stream

Getting out you shake my hand,
it's as spongy as cotton spun
The elegance you show so courteous,
to not at all be outdone

I commence and bow to thank,
the welcome that you have sent
And with a pleasant nod and wink,
I know you consent

Again you have a word and giggle as though,
We're children once again
Inviting me to have a chat,
becoming more than friends

As the dark draws near
We share an alcohol of love.
This happening day is what I cherish
You are surely sent from above.

I Miss Myself

With the darkness in the shadow
Suffering effects of the cold,
Yet suffocated in the sweat,
I stumble down the road.

Being forced to follow what others crossed by,
Crime it is as if else I try,
Tears crosses the redness of my cheek,
And it's the only way my eyes speak,
Lips of mine when it turns dead.

I am happy I really try to,
To be smiling as if I was made to,
I shout of something I don't know
But there's what my inner self knows,
That's what my sparkling eyes speak,
And that's what ugly, untold but true,
Yes I feel,
Yes I understand,
I miss myself,
Yes I know!
Yes, it's true.
I miss myself.

Nikhil Chandwani

Love, Gives You Hopes

In the frosty of an ancient first light
That lazily lingers on;
Love, will give you hopes

In the middle of an intense storm
That trees you tattered and worn;
Love, will give you hopes

Even while your tears fall like rain
And your sour soul screams aloud
And you believe there's not anything missing to gain
As you walk lost in a crowd...
Love, will give you hopes.

When your heart begins to break
And you think, "No more can I take,"
Love, will give you hopes..

When need outweighs your means
And you have not anything left but dreams;
Love, will give you hopes.

Even while your tears fall like rain
And your sour soul screams aloud
And you feel there's not anything left to gain
As you walk lost in a crowd...
Love, will give you hopes

Soldiers After The Battle.

I hope my life within myself

To heal these war scars
But life at times unties itself
With slow and poisonous bars.

That pulls me back from freedom's grace
From the future I'd hoped to be
Enjoying with independent face.
In search of empty glee.

All my times since life begun
The constant fight surrenders
Often shows what strength has won
My life after the battle.

For This Instant Of Time

For this very instant of time
I held reality within my hand
I read the meaning beneath the eyes
And just began to understand

So many feelings are still mysterious
For this very instant of time
Yet motionless I know. I'm not alone
The boundary is crusty, still not define

In this humanity just passing through
Another branch in the tree line
For this very instant of time
I hope my clouds will live as blue
And when the heart of life will forever pause
I'll still remember love so kind
In position of prayer on knees I crash
For this very instant of time

Yaseen Anwer

Yaseen Anwer is the Founder and Managing Editor of poetry group "Poets Corner Group". He is widely published poet and has contributed for more than 70 national and international anthologies. Coming up with the innovative idea of publishing young aspiring poets with eminent personalities, this brainchild of his, has over 4000 members across the world and over 11 printed anthologies where the works of several amateurs have been published. Yaseen writes in Hindi and English and the group promotes poetry in both languages. He also has had the honour of having his words translated to other languages like Chinese, Portuguese, Hindi, etc.

Born in Patna in a middle class household with his father working as a doctor and mother as a homemaker, He believes poetry is the best expression of emotions and started reading and writing poetry at the age of fourteen getting inspired by poets such as Rabindranath Tagore and Mirza Ghalib. Encouraging newer talents in poetry and publishing them alongside renowned poet-personalities like Dr.A.P.J Abdul Kalam, Ruskin Bond, Vikram Seth, Gulzar, Irshad Kamil, Kapil Sibal, Shashi Tharoor, Deepti Naval, Shekhar Kapur etc. he has enabled the dreams of many like him to be fulfilled and have made them feel to be a part of the bigger picture. Recognizing his talent and effort in the field of poetry, he was awarded with the "Young Poet Award 2012" by Indian poetry society.

Mourning

Let
Me be free
From part of me
That
I no longer
Wish
To be recognized

Let
Memories cry
Fade and die
An ageless mourning
Invokes
Restless soul
To seek an endless sleep

Let
My feelings
Scream
Only then
You will realize
It's not a
Forbidden dream.

Yaseen Anwer

<u>Nothing Ends, Nothing Stays</u>

Nothing ends
Nothing stays
Each end
Promises new beginning
And each beginning
Promises new end.

End of shore
Promises beginning of the sea
And beginning of the sea
Promises another shore.

Dawn of night
Promises beginning of new day
And beginning of new day
Promises another night.

Each foetus delivered
Promises beginning of new life
And beginning of each new life
Promises grave some day.

Nothing ends
Nothing stays
Each end
Promises new beginning
And each beginning
Promises new end.

Waseem A Malla

Waseem A Malla is a poet from Srinagar (Kashmir) , northern part of India. He has made attempts with different genres of poetry in English, Urdu and Kashmiri. His poetry is generally romantic in nature, though superficially, but within a deeper perspective, his poems depict a thrust on mystical elements, with a representation of Asian philosophy. His poetry has been deeply influenced by the contemporary Urdu poetry and this thing can be well established by reading most of his poems. His writings are mostly influenced by Agha Shahid Ali, Ahmad Faraaz,

Waseem A Malla

Parveen Shakir and Mewlana Jalal-ud-Din Rumi. At present, he is working as the Managing Editor of a quarterly eMagazine 'Fragrance' (efragrance.weebly.com) . His poems have been published in a no. of anthologies, of which 'Fiesta of Love', 'Moods & Moments', The Art Of Being Human vol.6 and 'Aatish' (coming soon) require a special mention. One of his poems is part of a novel 'Intelligence Code' Part 1.

Adieu: A Farewell

Tonight as I watch you go, perhaps forever,
I can see face of moon gloomy and sad,
And all stars weeping bitterly around it,
For I may not hold your hand for long,
And ask you to stay, just one more time,
As choices for me have turned to ashes,
So have been all emotions I held within,
In my heart, embossed infinitely deep in it.

Bidding my farewell to this love I stand,
All alone as if in a vast desert, limitless,
Holding tears, waiting for rain from a cloud,
To hide my tears, when and if they flow-
My eyes are as sere as sand under my feet,
So seem to me all heavens over my head,
As they have endured same fate always,
As every night they part away since eternity

Waseem A Malla

It Is: A Ghazal

Look at my love, how grand it is,
So green a crop, in Heart's land it is;

Of all in existence, God thus spoke:
He commands it to 'Be', and it is;

Scars of my heart, what renews it so?
I wonder, whether salt or sand it is!

Castles of reality so shattered as sand,
Palace of fantasy! Look, how grand it is!

You watch my body shiver when I err,
Into filthy soul, my sacred errand it is;

Expect scars on Earth's face to fade away!
Wish in Mida's touch, a God's wand it is!

A friendless one you name self, Waseem!
Wiping your tears, whose bruised hand it is?

Desperation

One day, as I would look back,
Into my life lived all the days,
The days without you, and the nights,
Without any sleep comporting my eyes.

Those days, when I decided to call you,
Call you back into my life-
But was it my voice that failed me?
Or the air, the resisted to flow?

Those days, when I dreamt of you,
Of only you, within me, in my life-
But was it my sleep that faded?
Or your images that became blurred?

And the days, I decided to follow,
To follow you, to be united with you-
But were those my steps getting heavy?
Or was it the path that became untreadable?

All those nights, when I wanted to hug you,
To hug you, forever, safe in my arms-
Were those arms too weak to hold on?
Or was the distance too large to be safe?

All those nights, all those nights,
Haunted me; these days, these days-

What is it that lets me not sleep?
That lets me not to dream?

For every lone moment of my life,
It is no life I have lived, alone-
Is it you, or your love haunting me?
Or is it my hope leading to despair?

Journey Sans Destiny

I had set upon a journey, far and long,
For years I travelled with my luck along;

A journey, one of a thousand distances,
One look and tired felt all my glances;

With me, of seven colors, were my dreams,
And treaded along, of hope, few gleams;

Even not a single destination became mine,
Proposed I, but disposed the divine;

My hand gained not any color of rainbow,
In utter dark, faded every single glow;

As in a short flash after a thunder,
All my dreams were torn asunder;

The destination was destiny not for me,
My courage failed me, luck favored barely;

The judgement and the reward- were all yours,
So was the hazy, stoney untreaded course!

I returned home just a tired wayfarer,
My dreams, my hope- all lost in despair;

And my heart's longing for all eternal mirth,
Ended in adopting every sorrow of earth.

Lend Me

Lend me a little room in your eyes,
And dream of me just one night;

Lend me little space in your thoughts,
And think of me just for one flash;

Lend me a corner of your mind,
And memorize me just one more time;

Lend me a hand till I live my life,
And then touch me to bless immortality;

Lend me the scent of your breath,
And let the spring be my slave;

Lend me the fragrance of your body,
To perfume the roses in the fall;

Lend me the smile of your lips,
And see me rejoice all life long;

Lend me the jingle of your voice,
To defeat the birds best in their chirping;

Lend me the twinkle of your eyes,
To prevail over the stars of dark skies;

Lend me the brilliance of your face,
To show the moon: how to beautify;

Lend me all the virtues you have,
And show me how to praise the divine..!!!

Lovita J R Morang

Lovita J R Morang is a remarkably talented and multifaceted personality with interests in poetry, arts, films, media and TV. A graduate of Guwahati University, she did a short-term course on film appreciation from FTII, Pune, and has a post-graduate Diploma in Mass Communication from IGNOU. Lovita published a book of poems Storms in my Heart, 1996, and served as a Journalist for a year in the English Newspaper, The North-East Observer in 1997. Presently, she freelances, contributes Write-ups and poems for Assam Tribune English Daily. She has been a professional filmaker,artist,poet. She started filmaking early at the age of Twenty. And have made more than Twenty Documentaries, travelogue, tele-films. And her film titled" Virgin Rhododendron burnt alive" is recorded as the FIRST FILM on Climate Indicator Wildflower Rhododendron. She has pioneered the Fashion Industry in NE-India since 1993. She has acted in a number of movies and TV serials. She was the lead artiste in the Assamese feature film 'Morome Morom jane' and acted in 'Asene Kunubai Hiyat.' She acted as a princess in a docu-drama on massacre of Royal dynasty of Nepal produced by BBC Channel, London directed by Clive, 2005.Casted as Protogonist for Sandhiya Sundaram's short celluloid Cinema-DOREMIFA,and -n the absence of presence by Dominique produced by FTII,Pune and Satyajit Ray Film Institute,Kolkatta. Among many TV serials, she acted in 13-episode serial directed by national Award winner, Gautam Bora.

Lovita has produced and directed docu-film 'Boon By the Bond' on International relations through trade for PPC, Prasar Bharati, Doordarshan, 2008. She produced, directed and scripted 'The First Man-Jimchane,' a folktale of Mishimi Tribe for Prasar Bharati, Doordarshan, Itanagar, 2008. She also produced, directed and scripted docu-film on social tourism "Swarga Sa Sundar Ek Safar", 2006. Similarly, she has been involved with several other creative projects in the film and TV industry. She has many an anthology on poetries published worldwide with eminent poet of the world. Her aim is to dedicate herself in creating & communicating humanitarian messages through print and visual media.

Lovita J R Morang

Guise

Dawn pollinates
Wind blows angel's trumpet
In unit of force
tiniest life smiles

Drifting driftwood
Blindened by
speck of light

Humming birds floats in fogged Enchanted forest

Communal carnage
Ripped apart the fortress of fortune

On ruins
Love travels along hearse

Not to fear love
Hatred is
Who shall not hark

Call me once

Emptiness is a sign of no loss
I lost my feeling as a nihilist
I value still nothing

To reach for the noxious nectarine
Non-existent dies in mortal sin

in mortification I chant open sesame

A morn
in every glorious guise born

Lovita J R Morang

As Others

Centuries of burnt
Camphor burns
Reverbs on the wall
Blackening bastion of basilisk
Transforming and forming a breathing pattern
How far do we go back
Aping

Immersed in love
Everything has hardened the fragility of love
Grafting growing barriers

Timelessness stunted
Intensely push out to bolster being
Being loved is reaching out
Basmitzvah
Ceremonised to menstruate over the domino effect
Events of hatred and humiliation
Humbly be not invective

We live
With difficulties to keep alive
Endlessness is not stopping
Quit not for the quest
In no place
Rehearse to expand in new market
As I read new market

Accessibility
Challenges nothing
In the greatness we linger
Lost in Qualm
We lived a passion

Regression
In constant interplay
Disturbances defines angst
The look within
Is the empty sculpture
How you treat your bodily form
In my happy stories
I dream of freeing novelty
To a newer nominations

I qualify I quack
In the quantum leap
What I reap
Except as an Indian
My identity is
as others
Same as others

Lovita J R Morang

Abbot Of Abattoir

Abbreviated in decorous bravura
It's my oblation to worship
In breech birth
I bathe in obligation

I tear out my deformities.
from mountainous hollow
Dark rock with obsidian glow
I avalanche down in my sudden search
As if lost in the ballad
of an awry avowed atheist

I uplift delayed tactic
Toning up; tuning up
Up and down
I find myself in my own deftness
I deny to shrink not to deafness

To hear
The screams from Abbot of Abattoir

While I
Deflower with Object d'art
Smallest of objects metamorphs
In oblivion of sleep

I am awaken

As star-studded idol
Made of stones and sands

Subversively I surrender
To sublimate
From airy being
to metallic being

Surrogated vigour sends me off
To an unconditional surrender
To a mere acceptance of
A Putative lover...

Desecrate

Being to becoming
Becoming to being
My fragmented thoughts
Becomes time

Waiting for the day
That never comes
That will never come
Not yet an illusion

For this being to go on
Grappled in speed of moving
Love takes form in formless faces
I am the love now

I don't repeat
But talking
Walking
Working

I repeat talking
I repeat walking
I repeat working
Not to stop....

To be the continuous
To be the time

I am because of you
I am a concept
I am the concept

Force me to
I am the force
Force for the time being
Force for the things of becoming
I am the fiddler now
Fiddling time

I am transparent
Parenting time
Running out of senses of time
I am numb now

You smoke
Finally, to disconnect
You drink
Finally, to disconnect
Participating in destruction

Finally, Forgetting
Not transforming
Not Going
Not Growing
In wronged anger
Killing, dismissing the bodily love
Becoming fierce fiend

Come out of limitedness
Come back from destruction

Move again
Becoming
Being
In holy totality
In formless finality

Deserters Diadem

What sparkles as dewy dawn
Deviates my dwelling
Is earth-shattering
Is ending of purpose

A replicated endearing smiles
I engage myself into turbulence
Ending everything-I desert
I decline as a despot

Their purple hearts
Has a replicated energy
That enervates purposeless
Descry dazzles of Diadem

Run for it

I am a devout raconteur
Just to tell you
I do not race along racism
I am in a rag-trade
To cloth your denuded renunciation
Derring-do
To denunciate
To undo

Aberrations' in your behaviour

I traded my unflinching
Deeper calling
Unheralded
Into deeper calling
I walked through unknown
People forgets people
Memories baffles the brain
Mind you
humane still hums

I descend from some cloud-music

I repay
When prayers fail

I replay
When my foothold frail....

Aman Jakhar

Aman Jakhar is a final year student of B.Tech in Computer Science He is a passionate reader and a book reviewer. He founded a literary website Read In Park, to fill the gap between writers and readers in 2012. He is a struggling writer and is trying to mark his presence in crowd of thousands of authors. He likes to pen down what happens around his life.
He is a prolific blogger @
http://iamanjakhar.blogspot.in/

Aman Jakhar

She Is No Prostitute!

The girl you see in the brothel,
Or meet on street,
The girl you take to the hotel,
Or wherever you meet . . .

You never know what lies behind her smile,
Sometimes just try to feel the pain she hides,
She doesn't do it, willingly
When enjoying her – you smile,
Satisfying you, deep inside her – she cries . . .

But no other way she has now to earn,
She too was happy before that day,
When her picture – perfect life took a turn,
Gang raped by her lover,
Society didn't leave her with any other place to stay . .
.

We see only what we want to see,
We hear only what we want to hear,
Life taught her to survive this way,
She didn't complain and had anything to say,

The girl you see in the brothel,
Or meet on the street,
Will you help to destroy that girl?

The girl you take to the hotel,
Or wherever you meet . . .
Will we help to save that soul?
Because –
She is no prostitute!
She is no prostitute!

Aman Jakhar

Beautiful Girl

You beautiful girl, residing in my heart,
With admirers a lot.
With curly hairs and lips so sweet,
And summers barely sixteen.
Our eyes met, and we need not to speak,
I read the words in your eyes.
In your heart, I got a moment to sneak,
Hunger of love, I saw and it can't be a lie.
Where you go, there resides happiness,
You turn sorrow into pleasure,
And you keep when you make any promise grew,
You're the one I wish to treasure.
Your love demanding eyes, your teeth of pearl,
Glow on your face and so soft as flower,
Many would have died and a lot would have fallen
for your smile.
Come to open sky! And let me show you meteor
shower.
What you doing here sitting all alone?
Waiting for someone? Who
Betrayed you making false promises,
And ditched you for someone else?

Seeking true love, wishing one to be there,
Across me, you came here,
Oh God! Don't look so deep into my eyes,

The body holding this soul, I have surrendered to you
– would die.

My eyes have said it all, to your demanding eyes,
Now let your lips frame in reply.
Just have faith in love – once more,
I promise you the sky!

I will make you forget, the love he faked,
Hold and embrace me within you.
Believe me, I will keep the promises, he escaped.
And I will make you live the love again!

Aman Jakhar

<u>Don't Forget Me</u>

I don't know one thing,
Without you, what would be my suffering?

When I look
at you beneath full moon casting its beautiful light,
When you'll be gone
What I would look at?
When I imagine
you playing in white snow, in the autumn from my
window,
when you'll be gone
what I would imagine?

It seems like everything that exists,
fog, darkness, smoke, storm
were feelings
that goes
toward the heart of you that wait for me.

And,
if day by day you stop loving me
I'll never stop loving you any little.

And If all of sudden
you forget me
A part of you
will die within you itself.

If you think me gone nuts,
the wind of your love
that makes my life go around,
and you think
of leaving me in between of nowhere
remember
that that day,
at that instant,
there will be no existence left of this wind
that carried love.

But
if anytime,
you feel that we are made for each other,
if at any moment,
you feel that no one can love you like I did,
if each day a teardrop
dares to touch your lips,
come back to me.
Oh my bliss . . .
Oh my wish . . .

You know what?
In me
all the desires you had left unfulfilled,
are waiting to be fulfilled
with the hunger of your love, my beloved.
Just don't forget me.

Aman Jakhar

Pain Without You

I know you're gone,
But life would move on.
My heart is broken,
And so is your place in it.
I have lost you forever,
And with that a part of me died within.
So much of emotions I want to express,
But no one is here except my emptiness.
Because you were the one, with whom I used to fight,
And I am dying, just for your mere sight.
I've never felt more suicidal,
Even my tears have dried.
If I had a gun,
Definitely I would have tried.
Everyone around me have seen me broken,
With bowed head and lowered eyes.
She might be seeing me from skies,
I've spent my days and night with soulful cries.
Love, come and take me with you,
My pain of losing you is massive. It will go
Nowhere, but besides you, as I now sigh
Nowhere but in your arms, as I now die.

Wait

I don't want to live,
But I will . . .
I know it will be just,
For you . . .
Without you . . .
I don't wish to breathe,
But I will . . .
Because of you,
For you . . .
Without you . . .
I will be waiting,
Till the eve of my life . . .
Till the darkness don't arrive . . .
I will strive . . .
For you . . .
Without you . . .
Look the wonders of my dreams,
The thoughts of my wishes,
The gleam in my eyes,
The soul with my heart,
They still think!
You were my life,
But you're gone,
And I believe you will come back,
For me . . .
With me . . .
You were my happiness,

Aman Jakhar

And I will be happy again,
As you will be with me,
For me . . .
With me . . .
Nothing is going to be true,
That also I know.
But whenever I close my eyes,
I still wait . . .
I still pray . . .
You will be mine,
You will be back,
For me . . .
With me . . .
Forever again . . .

Sadia Khan

Strong believer in the religion of Romanticism, Sadia Khan, calls herself a true Bohemian by her pretty little heart. Dreamer as she evidently is, she fondly shaped her dreams into words and rhymes. A poet, a short story writer, Who loves to pen down the thoughts and the problems one usually gets while into a relationship. Also working as a relationship counselor at an online counseling organization — Wizpert, talking with the clients from all overthe world to help them resolve their personal issues and create even more love and indulgence in their depressed lives. An

Sadia Khan

avid blogger, too, who has already published more than hundred Poems and a few number of relationship oriented articles and short stories on her blog, Crescendoing Silence (http://sadiakhanainy.blogspot.in/)
Presently she is working on her two books- one of her own, and another with a co-writer.

Night-Traveler

The deeper I dissolved
How shallow it is
I realized
The depths I fathom now
Are nowhere near the sky
A long distance to go
Under the gaze of sleepy flies
Chirping of insects
Keep my entrancing sleep at bay
Stars are the guardian of ages, and
Moon, the protector of the way
If ever, had it been in my sight
Would have I ever known —
Nights have so much to say
Secrets unveiled only to a traveler
I shall have walked this trail
Till the night has received me as
A listener to those tales!

Sadia Khan

<u>Gibbous Moon</u>

Let not fury rob away my moon;
Hath it not been my lover akin?
Dissolving against the cool breeze
Damp dew preening its crude skin
Pretty waning gibbous moon is it?
Or some deep agony glorifying ye?
One drop of tear that God shed
Or, my mistress' misery hath escape
Frolic angels and simmering demons
They'd make the moon prettily drape
Draped as moon, my lover hath always
Cascades of pale yellow raw silk, and
Hollowed grey as her cheeks, chenille lace
My mistress would be my Rose Moon
Walking down the aisle in full June!

Thirsty Leaves

You knew of her love
And the autumn knew it, too
How she adored wandering
On the fallen sun-dried leaves
The crisp crunch of their skin
And the sound of her own steps
Forever endured her deepest heart
World around her would hush
And the earth played its flute
Yellow leaves danced in rhythm
Whilst everything has fallen mute
Here now, so wonderfully
You burn her with those leaves
And turn her into sallow ashes
If only, you would've known
Her solace abounded perfectly
And, her thirst forever parched
Not for burning with the leaves
But in blossoming with you!

Sadia Khan

~*Ameen*~

Look here,
O' my lovely sapphire
Grass is not so green
Ember is perfectly home
To the cozy warm pyre
Let me comb and preen
Your sun-tanned curls
Sit here, O' my lady lean
Open your amber eyes
To the sparkling snow, and
To the symmetrically frozen brooks
Look here, to the sky so sheen
For elves and imps had (s)wept
Those whimpering clouds clean
Whilst you slept
And were deceitfully kept
O' my pale queen
Color of your cheeks
Flushed to quagmire
Cocooning into an abyss of chaos
By the magic so keen
But, now your grim fate furrows
Cause, the same grass is no green
Sedated are bayous and meadows
And, the slumber, hypnotic and so mean,
Of no choice, now weans and mellows
Sweet demise of them, thither it weens

For dark blooms, and light shadows
O' my precious, look here into the unseen
What else wasting of a life hence endows
O' my love, look here, to what they'd glean,
And for once and last, say again, 'Ameen'!

Sadia Khan

When I'am Gone

Soon shall light be sucked away
From the only window
Sun glided once through
My withered skin, and
Rusted hope, akin
Thee shall find them stacked
Behind the closed door
In the leeway of thy smile
For it's the sun in thine eyes
And my smoldering tears
That'd only make me alive
Salvation not a mere myth,
My soul shall yearn for it
Smile and liberate my heart
For I beseech thee, one last time
A few fresh thorn-less roses,
And a last stale goodbye,
Find them in the attic
When I'm gone!

Rohan Kachalia

A Sagittarian by nature and hence hopelessly romantic by heart (termed by his wife) which he begs to differ, a banker by vocation, a blogger by leisure pursuit and an aspiring writer.

Have been taken to reading and blogging since last one year and reading and writing romance seems to be his forte, along with poems, haiku and erotica.

His only dream is to see himself as a successful author and 'Minds @Work 2' is the stepping stone for his dream to come true. He blogs jointly with his wife at: http://ponderingtwo.blogspot.in

His mantra for life is : Cheers, Keep Smiling & Embrace Love.

Rohan Kachalia

That Defining Moment

That moment of seizing a coy glance
The lovely gaze where eyes meet for a flash
Where heart skips a beat to dance
As ardent glee escapes with a panache

The loose strands of silk caressing her cheeks
Igniting the urge to feel thee
Her voluptuous lips flaring my inner at peaks
That heartily threatening my sanity

A firm handshake followed by the sweet melody of
her influence
As thoughts got exchanged, agreed to and doubled
Every second's every minute's soothing cadence
Ray of future got candled

Beauty's effect without brain doth not excel
And a 'Yes' with a nod of heads is where Love doth
dwell

Concupiscent Desire

Eyes staring at each other
Leaving a pixie at both ends

Distance went dangerously minimizing
As they started exploring their intimacy

It was nothing short of a pipe dream
Feeling the softness of fur under the moon light

Hearts did a simultaneous somersault
As excitement reigned

Foremost a tinge, igniting the desires
When bodies pressed against each other's in time

A summer zephyr stroked each other's hair
Cherishing the warmth generated

With a beseech in eyes
To Love more

Wild passions and emotions ran deep
With kisses and more kisses and even more kisses

Nothing could stop them today
As every touch, every kiss felt insufficient

Eventually leading to a tighter embrace
Of hearts, of souls and minds under the moon light

Knot of Love

Love doth dances thou to its tune
Everything seems eternally beautiful
Reasons and explanations stand jejune
As thou follow heart's desire akin to a bible

Thy lips widens anon
Upon that beautiful vista
Yesterday seems aeon
Howbeit today thy hearts danced to its raga

Thou gramercy at parent's denial
Thy choice doesn't interest
As luck scripted the fable
Quotha turned out to be commonest

They carved thee for him with a hallelujah
As thou tie the knot with thy heart's diva

Nehali Lalwani

Nehali Lalwani, born an brought up in Nadiad, Gujarat. She has done Masters in Human Resource Management from Sardar Patel University. Currently she is working as an Assistant professor at N.S Patel Arts College, Anand. She is sociable, playful and enthusiastic by nature. She loves writing. She believes it is zeal; an urge; something that gives her an opportunity to express herself. She writes when she is happy; when she is furious or when any issue strokes her heart. The theme of Love finds a new definition in her stories. Her philosophy of life says that love though unfulfilled it never dies. She has good collection of poems and short stories on different emotional genres. Recently her short story got published in Kaleidoscope by Parlance Publishers along with that recently her 2 poems got published in Moods and moments- Poetry book by Writers Empire, She has also worked in an anthology Syahi as an Writer and Co Editor. Besides all she loves to read love stories and listening Music in her spare time.

Nehali Lalwani

I Made A Friend

I made a pal, someone new,
I heed his lexis as vocal true,
How swiftly did the era go past,
I thought I had initiate love at last.

Until one day of dim dejection,
I look for him, he wasn't there,
Distress crammed my wrecked heart,
I thought as a fool right from the start

Endless qualms have crammed my head,
As I lay lament in my bed,
Will he ever tell me why,
That this was just some cruel lie.

I know his days are mixed up bad,
Hard choices for him in tears are clad,
I lay here battered and offended deep,
Wonder if his word he'll keep.

He promised he'd always be my friend,
Love me till time does end,
Will he catch me as I fall,
Or witness me collapse after all.

I'am A Woman

I will always meet you halfway,
But won't go alone all the way.

I will walk next to you,
But I will not just pursue you.

I will appease your harm,
But I will not hurt myself of course.

I will care for you,
But I will care for myself too.

I will cry for you,
But I will not cry because of you.

I will save you from yourself,
But I will not lose my part in you.

I will never leave you,
But I will not be left.

I will hold you when you need me,
But I will not let you hold me down.

I will give as much as you do,
But I will not let myself be taken .

Nehali Lalwani

I will allow your imperfections,
But I will not let myself to be insulted.

I will endure your pain,
But I will not let myself be abused.

I will love you more,
But I will not be loved any less.

I will let you be a *man*,
But I will never forget I am a *Woman*.

I Wish...

I wish I were an angel
To submerge your globe with my glow
To grasp, soothe and relieve you
All through long lonely night

I wish I were a fairy
To flutter about your precious heart
To confer tiny clutches
When you are about to fall apart

I wish I were a goddess
Of beauty a paragon
So you would stare and marvel
Belief of any added one

I wish I were a muse
Alive there within your psyche
To offer inspiration
When precise lexis you want to find

I wish I were a princess
Sacred with lavishness so fine
I'd make you live in splendor
If you give your word to be mine

I wish I were a star
Sprinkling stardust down on you

Nehali Lalwani

Guiding each and every step
Make your darling wish come true

I wish I were the moon
Running on your inner tides
Drawing you ever closer
Till in me your love abides

I wish I were the sun
Burning to the very core
Blazing you with my obsession
Emission stirring what I adore

I wish I were a flower
To blossom and nurture by your care
Enfold you in my fond fragrance
Craft life beautiful and fair

I wish I were the wind
Embracing you each way
Wrapping you in my arms
Seductress having my way

I wish I were the rain
That soaks body through and through
That sprinkles love dewdrops on you
But then beats itself on you

I wish I were the sea

Bubbling, whipping delight
To depict you into my deepness
Riding waves, set free and free

But I am just a woman
I'm as simple as I can be
But if you give me your love
All these marvels you will see

Memories

The sweetest thud of blazing trees
A gentle spanking in the wind
Silence has lasted past the storm
Gloomy dreams and Satan's growl

Too many vistas conceded my mode
A time found lone in the mist
The softest screeches are running strip
My aching bones squeak as I stare

You walk a distance towards me
The fall's eternal, can you see
I'm reminiscence in your heart
I whisper to you in the dark

The battle's started at the end
No one is coming to regret
The sinners seized their wine from prey
No verdict call here to stay

The game is reckless to be told
The one is laughing at his souls
It falters nowhere to be sure
The power grows forever more

Like a spirit in the storm
I have to say in where you've been

But cross the line to come to me
And pay the price for ecstasy

You walk a distance towards me
The fall's eternal, can you see
I'm reminiscence in your heart
I whisper to you in the dark

Nehali Lalwani

I Bet...

At times I think of what it could be
I think of all the ways I could amend,
And I See the possibility...

At times I like to be alone
In wintry and forlorn room,
And I'd think about tomorrow...

Don't judge me since I'm diverse to you,
Don't stare at me since I'm not like you,
Don't curse me as I created myself
And as you still tracing for the fact!

Today, today I bet my life
The whole thing will alter
Because of what I have in me...

Today, today I wonder
why you have no idea
what I've put aside me...

Don't stare at me like you don't know who I am
Since I created myself,
Since I have a reason to smile
And a reason to live my life...

Don't condemn since you aren't better

Think of all the things we've done together,
And find it in your heart to be content
All I want is you to feel truly content...

Since today is the day
I will fling this chaos away,
I'll clean up my space
throw all my old dirty shoes away...

Since from now on I'm diverse
And there is no way,
I will twist on my words
Like I always said and did before...

Today, today I bet my life
You have no idea
What passed through my mind...

And today, just today I found out why
why you hate me so much by
all the times I smile...

You can be happy darling
why can't you be?
You can be happy my love
but not with me...

You can be like a gratis bird
Why give that up?
We are all free
from the very start.

Nehali Lalwani

Lt Col. Ankita Srivastava

A courageous, bold, hardworking and dedicated lady who by her strong sense of discipline has always challenged her potential and have set varied targets for herself.

She served the nation as an able Army Officer displaying her strength and stamina and hung the uniform after eventful innings of full fourteen years to don the civvies while again serving the nation through the banker to every Indian- the State bank of India.

She gives wings to her mental passions by constantly penning down her over-exuberant heart; be it in the form of a novel, short story , ghazals or poetry. She has a grip on expression of depth and knows how to play the game of 'words'. Poems have been her first love.

Two decades back she had composed 40 poems out of which one had made a proud place in American Poetry Anthology. Some were published in 'Sarita', 'kadambini', 'Manorama', 'Grihashobha' ,'Jetset' and many english local newspapers of Allahabad. Almost all her poems were broadcasted on AIR in the youth programme 'Uvvanai'.

She believes every beating heart is a poet- a dormant poet; only initiatives like Minds at Work 2 can turn them into active volcanic poets.

Lt Col. Ankita Srivastava

Perfect evening

It was a perfect evening
Full of all meaning
Tasteful as it was
Moving slow,
But without a pause
Steaming and beautiful
Undeniably very wonderful.
The shine and glitter
Was making me quiver
I wonder how I didn't get lost
No; I think I did get lost.
The food, the drink and
You, made my soul drenched
Just in that small moment
My lifetime's thirst got quenched.
From that perfect evening, what I carried back with
me,
I am still holding since so many years.
They might have been just your words, you see,
For me,
It was your love shining against my ears!

<u>Your Lips</u>

I never happen to consider
Your lips to be of some wonder
But this I came to realise,
My heart, mind, soul and body came to life;
When to your lips, I had my first touch
It felt - it put an end to my search.
It was as if you had fired
Hot and caring sensations.
My lips you had conquered
It was best of all the presentations.
I wonder what you felt
Something surely nice
Not watching your motions melt
As shut were my blushing eyes!
After that you kissed me so many times
Turning me nuts at all times
Always filling me with love and affection
Making me reach the heights of perfection.
Soon I'll be going very far from your touch
But I'll think about your face so much-
So much that I'll end up in thoughts
Shaking my ribs
Each time whenever I'll think about your great lips!

Lt Col. Ankita Srivastava

I am in Love

'What is love?'
This very question always brought
my brows closer
with my lips twistingly ready to answer-
'Fools indulge themselves
in this foolish act
and its never gonna make
over me any impact
Definition whenever asked ,
I never had a comment to pass
Simply shrugging the idea with indifference,
Considering it a thing of sheer unimportance.
Laughing always at the sight of lovers,
Calling stupidity their unusual behaviour.
Against the topic folks often heard me debating
"its a waste of time" they saw me firmly stating.
I would've continued with that attitude
Had you not shadowed me by your magnitude.
I would have been a total solivagant
Unneeded to anyone, with a life- vacant.
I wonder why I was so badly wrong
When now I discover tis' only Love that I long.
The behaviour of lovers would've never been
amusing
Had I known I'd be much badly behaving.

A Kiss from You

I brush my teeth, wash my face,
And look in the mirror-
I see you.
At that time early in the morning,
What I need is-
Just a kiss from you!
I try to touch your face
As I lean against that basin space.
You're smiling at me
You're teasing me
You're holding me
You're releasing me
Slowly and slowly warmth has enveloped
I notice some cold feet, I have developed.
I close my eyes -
I want the moment to stay,
'I Love You' ... I hear you say.
The warmth turning to heat now,
My body is shaking don't know how,
Can I regulate inflow of your passions?
Can I stop outflow of my emotions
I know soon I will be lost
Should I be greedy at this cost?
I open my eyes to stop the wave,
I realise I have to switch off the hot water to save.
I look in the mirror again-
I don't see you

Lt Col. Ankita Srivastava

> Yet I become greedy again,
> For a kiss from you!

Untitled

You contemplate to me quite easily
"Try to forget "
But you don't realise
How much it is difficult-
For I think of you every moment
Of my existence
And to forget you-
I have to go into Non-Existence.
If I think of you all the time
How can I forget you in my lifetime.
We may have jointly decided
Not to cross each other's way
We may have sworn not to see
Each other anyday
But darling how will you stop me
From travelling through the air;
And reaching your heart how over you would hide it
deep in layer
So all your orders to me- to be strong
is breaking anyway
Forgetting is far off, I am coming closer
to you day by day.

<u>Soham Majumdar</u>

Originally from Kolkata, currently residing and working in Delhi. His father is a retired medical representative. Soham has an elder sister who is a professional painter, now residing in the USA. She is married.

Presently he is working as a Director, Content and Strategy Development, with Value 350 Communications. Prior to joining Value 360 communications he has worked with a few MNC PR firms like Weber Shandwick, Text 100 Global Public

Relations, Perfect Relations and Genesis Burson Marsteller handling the corporate mandates for HP, EMC, Cisco, Bharti Walmart etc. In all, he has around 6 years of experience in the PR industry. He loves to travel, prepare new cuisine and write blogs, poems, articles ET all. Soham completed his education from Hans Raj College, Delhi University. He always had a knack for creativity, content writing and generating ideas and that is what he does now, for a living. He is a friendly, simple and down-to-earth person who draws happiness from simple things in life.

Soham Majumdar

Love

What is love?
Is it a bliss or a curse?
Is it a conductor to happiness
For a weathering and decaying life.
Or an insulator to the same

What is love?
Is it a dream or a nightmare?

What is love?
Is it the sound of the rustling leaves?
Exposed to the cool west wind,
Or is it the dull muffled noise
Of the wintry branches
Exposed to the dark stormy night?

What is love?
Is it a cyclone of ecstasy?
Or is it a whirlpool of relentless pain?

Now characterize the anatomy of love- Confused?

<u>How Many Times...</u>

I wandered through the strips of unceasing prairies,
I sailed to the nadir of limitless horizons,
I tossed a leaf in the breeze,
Just to see where it sashays to…

I watched the mist covered mountains in the vicinity,
I watched the silver ocean wave
Splash against the rock under the waxing moon
I listened to the song bird
Hmm a sweet melody on the tree by the brook,
My eyes loitered beyond the horizon
To a world of magic and miracles

I wished to turn back time,
From twilight to dawn.
Little did I realize that
Life is engulfed in slow decay.
The coldness grew, dreams turned to ashes,
Never to rise as a phoenix again,
Destiny turned away, never to return as fate again.

I counted how many times,
I managed to smile through tears,
How many times I weaved hopes through sorrows,
How many times I swam against the tides,
Just to find myself struggling in the same place again.

Soham Majumdar

How many times I tried to build a palace out of
broken bricks,
How many times I tried to paint doves on a white
canvas,
How many times I tried to reach out to you!

Hope

As I wandered through the serpentine by-lanes of life,
Each of my footsteps seemed to find itself
Getting engulfed in to a maze of sorts,
I relied on memories and looked back at the bygone
years,
To derive a cue from and to stride ahead,
I unravelled a void- A magnanimous stretch of
torturous void.

Many a times I have looked up
At the stars and asked a quiver full of 'whys?'
And "what ifs",
But the answers have been
Just another equally evasive question.
Hopes and dreams, the most innocuous of ambitions,
Seemed to traverse through a self imposed change
In identity; an identity- Obnoxiously ambiguous.

Times have changed, the essence hasn't,
I still find myself in an elusive clutter of obscure
rendition of happiness,
Groping for a sign of trust,
Seeking love in the indifference of touch,
Seeking warmth in the coldest of smiles,
And holding on to that same innocuous ambition,
Waiting for it to transform into a beloved reality!

Soham Majumdar

Words Which Means More Than Just Words

Whenever I listen to music that touches my soul,
It reminds me of you,
Whenever I see the moonlight seep thru the trees at
night,
Playing hide and seek with the shadows of the day
That had just passed by; it reminds me of you,

You have made me fragile as glass
But that same glass makes life seem so beautiful to
me.
If words could explain what u mean to me,
I wouldn't mind delving into
Etymology to discover that word…

Prateek Singh

An engineering graduate from Ghaziabad, Uttar
Pradesh currently working in a Noida based e-
learning Company, respire some fresh air being a
poet, an avid blogger and an enormous Nature lover.
He is the man with limitless imaginations, fanciest
dreams, musing mind, sentimentalist heart, peace
loving soul. He loves to be lost in rhythms. He loves
to get along with words. He firmly believes that
relationships go a long way if we put our true heart
within them. He possesses transcendental approach

towards life. He value things that are kept aside often and lot more of me yet to come if you want to know. He loves to Interact with different kind of people, Singing, Penning Indulging himself into WORDS.

A Moonless Night

A fatigued being
just rambled on endlessly
unless I found a dream,
a dream that shoved me
into a moonless and lonesome night
rhythmical strings of my harp
got snapped
out of the blue,
I freed myself
from those trammels
and shone the way
I ever longed for,
Those ephemeral joys
renders an everlasting contentment
within me,
I quaffed the serenity of still
and it knocked me out,
This is how
the tranquility infused
that surreal disposition within me,
Though it was a moonless night
It was so evident yet
like never before.

Prateek Singh

Dwindling Fantasy

By all means
I toiled
but the sand slipped through
my intact hands,
I craved to be
as free as those insane waves
of a shore less ocean
but my arid heart
could not hold
a few moist remembrances
Ah!
I can foresee that
naked horizon
caressing winds
moaning moon
stimulating eventide
I am imploringly
getting drowned
deeper and deeper
into the realm of
a mesmerizing fantasy.

The Treader Of A Lonesome Path

Acquainting with multitudes
endearing a few,
yearning for lying on the petals
like the dream of a dew,
I tread on a lonesome path.

Warding the thorns off
paving the way out of the gloom,
embracing the vicissitudes
I tread on a lonesome path.

Swinging between heights of elation
and depths of dismay,
trying to fall on the middle path,
but failing to do so repeatedly
having a song of karma on my lips
I tread on a lonesome path.

When my grey sun shines
my ego outshines,
When I want to follow the righteousness
I myself just obliterate the signs,
keeping my straying steps intact
I tread on a lonesome path.

I get hurt when I see this
irrational exuberance,

just think why do we adore
this material influence,
but the floating beads can't
make a necklace,
rather all the beads need
to have that perseverance,
absorbing all the plunges and soars
I tread on a lonesome path.

An occult keeps guiding me
those scriptures keep preaching me,
notwithstanding my waning vitality
I keep seeking for the supreme bliss,
chanting those divine rhymes
I tread on a lonesome path.

Entangling with the luxuries,
getting ignorant with the rationality
we are tending to forget
the power of ONE,
rekindling the belief of fire,
I tread on a lonesome path.

A Crescent Moon

Vying with innumerous hopes
a thing goes on glittering
proving itself a balm on
so many wounds
twitching with some losses, but
intimating a few vital gains
soothing thousands souls
inspiring too many hearts
witnessing some great arrivals
saying 'adieu' to some departures
starting the signs of darkness,but
bringing out a new dawn to live in
its nothing but
a crescent moon,
roams all around for some
stands still for a few
its nothing,but
a CRESCENT moon..

Prateek Singh

A Musing Walker

Staring into the blank
I felt like scampering
out of the blue
perhaps that vacuum
too got sick of my solitude
even those vacuums too have some
craving eyes with them after all,
So I had a thought
to walk on
and its a solitary walk,
While walking
something popped in my mind
it was like
although anybody is not that good
at answering thing
yet life raises countless questions
But we are here
to find out those answers
aren't we..??
This is another thing
how life takes them
but we should keep trying..
At times
questions indemnify things
even then we are the one
who have to wear a smile
on the face and a lasting twitch

in the soul simultaneously
again we are left alone
with this stoicism,
We get screened out
for we are not up to the mark
so...
is that all sticking to the
success and failure
all the time?
Even a soulful effort
has got nothing to do at all
Once again we are left alone
with the outcome,
but in the end
our conscience makes the real difference
against all odds,
After all feet always make
walking possible and fruitful too
no matter who are you with
sometimes,
A walk unveils
so many mysteries
that life possesses between the sheets,
Moreover
I prefer to be
A Musing walker...

<u>Renu Sethi</u>

A homemaker, mother, blogger and an amateur writer/poet, who pens her observations, weird yet intriguing lives of real people with real problems. Renu is an avid reader and has written for publications including a Penguin anthology and an e-magazine named Storizen. She blogs at <u>http://day-to-daystories.blogspot.in/</u> about Love and Relationships. When she is not writing, she plays her role of a doting mother, wife and daughter to the hilt.

Life : Lets Make It Count

I sit on the footpath
I wonder what seem different
As I watch others and do the math
I see smiles that are still unspent

Everybody seems in a perpetual hurry
People running here and there
All they do is whine and worry
And call the god's gift (life) unfair

If only they could understand
Life is nothing but an adventure
And nothing in it is pre-planned
It's a risk of joint-venture

So lets just free ourselves
Move forward with a special hand in our hand
Jig-saw puzzle is all we need to solve
For all pieces to fall in place as planned.

Renu Sethi

<u>My Old Self</u>

In the middle of the crowd,
Still I feel alone
No one near me
I am my dark clone

I was nice
I was humble
I would laugh
Even when I stumbled

As I started to take
Seriously my life
I have shredded all the fun
With a serious' knife

I want my old self back again
But I don't know how
I don't want to run like animals
Not ever ....not Now

Moon and Me

Standing on the moonlit terrace
I do wait to see you in that glow
I want to melt in your embrace
Counting stars as the clouds flow

If clouds are my friends tonight
They'll help me when you come
Hide us in darkness as we unite
And witness as we become one

I'll wonder where you are now
I'll think of who are you with
As the fear of doubts come bare
I'll wonder if love is but a myth

Till you come, I sit on the terrace
With the moon smiling beside me
Till you, the love of my life, comes
And I can no longer feel so lonely

<u>Your Kisses Your Touch</u>

Everyday when I look into your eyes
I always feel I can't love you more
Every morning when I feel your warm hug
I know you are the man I would die for

And when my skin burns with your touch
I realize its your soft touch that allures
Every kiss of yours is a promise
Words that come out of your mouth are hard to
ignore

Every single minute without you is torture
Remember "you'll be always around" you swore
Would give anything to be in your arms
Would present you with all the kisses I have in store.

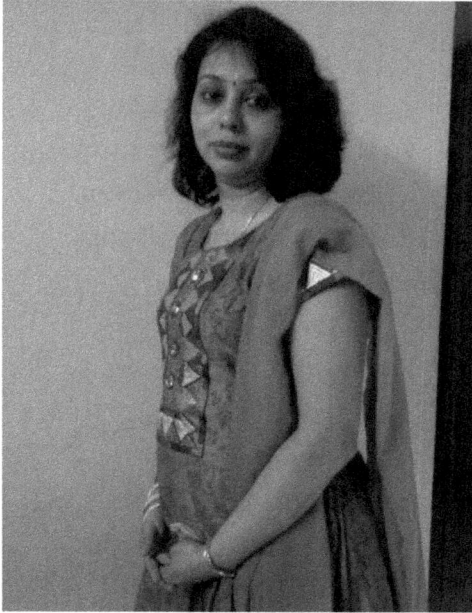

Janaki Nagaraj

Janaki Nagaraj is a graduate in English Literature yet, she did not discover her passion for writing till a couple of years back.

More than writing a prose, she found it easier to express herself through poetry. She is a full time homemaker and mother of two teens (that should say a lot about her patience) and lives in Mumbai. She blogs at http://www.janakinagaraj.com

Janaki Nagaraj

Enigma

I try to put a face
To the image in my mind,
I try to figure a person
Behind the voice I listen.
Who are you?
Are your eyes
Deep blue, like the sea....
Or black like the moonless night?
Is your smile wistful....
Or mischievous
When you think of me?
Is your hand rough....
Or will I turn jelly
As they touch me?
Do you like .....
To dance in the rain......
Or run for cover, when they do?
Are you a dreamer.......
Or a cynic
Do you still have the child in you?
Looking life with wonder and joy
Or too practical and grown-up...
Even to wonder?
Are you moved by
The beauty of nature............
Or are you removed from it?
Do you like it when

Wind ruffles your hair………..
Or are you ruffled by it?
Do your break into
A song of the season……
Or dance without a reason?
You are the thirst
I wanna quench;
You are the book
I wanna read;
You are an adventure
I wanna explore;
You are person whom
I wanna know to the core.
Will you ever reveal yourself
Or will you choose to remain an enigma to me?

Janaki Nagaraj

Vortex

Let me sleep on
If this is a dream,
Let me live on
If this is real.
Beauty was never
So beautiful,
Color so colorful,
Light so bright,
Night so painful.
Feels like I am a feather
So light that
I take flight
And soar with delight.
In this season of love
The heart blooms like a flower
Flutters like a fly
Warms up to a smile
Gallops at a thought.
Feels like being sucked
Into the vortex of a
Whirlpool, deep down
A abyss…black out!
Then, being thrown up
Into the eye of a storm
Pulled into a twister
Tossed about and
Free falling again.

Riding the waves of ecstasy
Doped on dopamine
Rocking and reeling
Drowning in passion,
These are the feelings
I never wanna grow out of!

Paradox

Heavenly showers quench the thirst
Of many a soul and this Earth
I welcome rains with open arms
It entices me with sensuous charm

I sit on the rocks by the sea
Water meeting Water is all I see
Two bodies merging to be one
Rapidly disappearing in the horizon

The rain drop kisses the Earth
She sizzles under this touch
Hasn't She been waiting for seasons
This alone is enough to reason

Soaked to the bone in this shower
Drenched with love of the lover
Down the body, water cascades
Tingling feelings of intense desire

Rains, supposed to quench thirst
Yet, makes you more thirsty
Waiting to embrace your Beloved
Thoughts that cloud, make you heady

The cool water kindles a spark
Gusts of wind ignites that fire
Lightening and Thunder add to the duel
Who said water couldn't fuel??

Janaki Nagaraj

Desert Strom

Alone in the desert
Middle of nowhere
Searching for direction
Leading to LaLa land
Rogue wind blows
Indicating a storm
The mind is in turmoil
Can I hide or run?
The force takes me by surprise
Leaves me gasping for breath
Searching to hold on to something
Preventing my fall down to earth
Wind rips me apart
Layer by layer
There I lay stripped,
Unmasked, with just a prayer
The worst has passed
Revealing my soul
Am I not still here
Without crying foul?
Stone becomes a diamond
Passing through the hell
Character reveals strength
When you come out of shell
Middle of the desert
Lying on the ground
Covered with sand

I have come undone
I stand straight
Head held high
I carry on walking
Without as much as a sigh!

Janaki Nagaraj

I Beleive...(About child sex slavery)

I was found in a gutter,
Cos' they don't need no girls,
I was sold and resold
Till I landed in this hell hole.
I die every day, many times
I've lost the count
Beaten, bruised and compromised
Times I don't wanna recount.
The well has dried up
So have my eyes
Cannot tell the difference
Between stone and I.
A faint whisper from the heart
To break free and live my part
I did dare to run away
Fought to keep the wolves at bay.
I live a LIFE now,
Carefree and strong
Believe in yourself
Cos' you are never wrong.

Vijayeta Tirkey Kataria

Vijayeta Tirkey Kataria hails from Assam and currently settled in Hyderabad. She has completed her Post graduation in Human Resource and has 6 years of experience in HR Spanning. In her leisure time she loves to compose poems, dance and cook different cuisines. Her poems have been published in newspapers, International Journal and books. She believes in living and enjoying each and every moment as there is only one life to live.

Vijayeta Tirkey Kataria

In Love

You enthralled me,
When I looked into your sparkling eyes.
The warmth in your smile,
Swept me off my feet.
Your tender touch,
Made me go weak in my knees.

You make me feel special,
By the things you do and say.
In your heart I find,
The love that lacked in mine

Wrapped in your arms, I feel safe,
Holding your hand I feel close,
Even when we sit in absolute silence,
It makes me blissful, just being by your side.

It's our destiny that we met,
And the mystic love has bonded us.
But sometimes I wonder, what we have is too good to
be true,
Am petrified to get my heart broken,
And too scared of the thought of losing you.

One Life To Live

Ailing and fragile I lay on the bed,
Thinking of the life spent,
Bustling, Hurrying was I always,
Travelling along life's busy way.

Snubbing the gifts offered,
Life seemed overbooked.
Forever I raced around,
Bemoaning there's no time.

With each breath I now lament,
How I took my loved ones for granted,
Ungrateful to people around,
Squandered opportunities to celebrate.

Death knocked the door, and I realized,
One life to live is what we have.
Longing for a second chance,
To embrace life and revel.

<u>Meghant Parmar</u>

Meghant Parmar hailing from New Delhi is a born car & gadget fanatic. His love for books blossomed when he first came across Tinkle & Champak magazines. Later on reading fiction became a forte and he is one of the fastest readers present around. He did his English Honors and now is looking for an opportunity to make a name for himself in writing industry. He is an upcoming book reviewer with a blog only dedicated to book reviews. His penchant for reading, writing and observing the surroundings comes naturally. He'll be making his debut in the

literary world with a short story co-authored with
Heena Ahuja in "Uff Ye Emotions-2". When he is not
writing and reading you can find him exploring
historical places and following cricket religiously. He
currently resides in Chennai.

You can contact him at meghantparmar@gmail.com

Meghant Parmar

<u>Life's Dilemma</u>

It's a gloomy night
Sleep nowhere in sight
The day not so bright
Searching for a ray of light.

Life has turned pale white
Emotions are slight
Hope turning into might
Searching for a ray of light.

Mind is in a fright
Feet swaying like candle light
Moments deprived of delight
Searching for a ray of light.

Everyday is a fight
With no upward flight
Standing at a height
Searching for a ray of light.

Determination pale like a plight
Sorrows not disappearing overnight
There goes again a night
Searching for a ray of light.

One day the time will be right
Shift in the luck will be slight
I'll be back in spotlight
With shine like sunlight.

Meghant Parmar

The Lost Soul

I feel like a shooting star
running away from the world.
I feel like smoke in the sky
Creating blackness in the life.
I feel like an unknown object
filling void in someone's life.
I feel like a helpless soul
Staring death in front of my eyes
I feel like a black spot
spoiling the party of happy lives.
I feel like I could hide
where there were no prying eyes.
I feel like I could cry
where tears could move hearts.
I feel like a lost child tonight
because there is no one my own tonight.
I feel like I could laugh aloud
To hide my sorrows in plain sight.
I feel like an old man
With too much wisdom at times.
I feel like a coward soul
When silence is my weapon.
I feel like running away
Because too many miseries galore.
I feel like a devotee tonight
Because god is on my side.
I feel like there is no one to listen

Because I'm far behind from time.
I feel the darkness around
When there is no ray of light.
I feel like I struggle a lot
When I don't have support at all.
I feel I could hold a hand
Which I could call mine.
I feel like going back in time
From where I could start again.
I feel I miss my close ones
Because I'm their dear every time.
I feel like I can sleep light
To forget all the sorrows with time.

Meghant Parmar

<u>Confessions of a lover</u>

When I was with you
My love knew no bounds.
When I was with you
My smile was like a shiny pound.

When I was with you
I conquered the battleground
When I was with you
My feelings for you were profound.

When I was with you
My heartbeats would resound.
When I was with you
Your words left me spellbound.

When I was with you
My sorrows went underground
When I was with you
My life just turned around.

When I was with you
My pleasures knew no bounds.
When I was with you
My body was completely astound.

When I was with you

My future would confound.
When I was with you
My love was truly found.

Meghant Parmar

Alone & Aloof

I was all alone
Struggling to be right
Few the choices I made
It left me high and dry.

I was all alone
surrounded by my plight.
Few steps did I take
It left me without a choice.

I was all alone
fighting to survive.
Few attempts that I made
It left me nowhere to hide.

I was all alone
trying to restore my pride.
Few advices did I take
It left me teary eyed.

I was all alone
wincing in the pain.
Few moments to calm me down
But it made me cowardice.
I was all alone
determined to set it right.
Few mistakes that I made

left me in the middle to die.

I was all alone
realizing it one night.
Few things that I let go
gave me the courage to survive.

Surbhi Thukral

Surbhi Thukral is a marketing professional turned writer. She has worked with corporations in India and the UK. After gaining success in business writing, she is determined to make a mark in the field of fiction writing. She has become a compulsive writer who dedicates many hours a day to fulfil her passion for creative writing. She holds Masters in Business & Management from the University of Strathclyde, UK. She can be reached at thukral.surbhi@gmail.com.

Her work has been published in the Harvests of New Millennium, January 2012; EWR: Short Stories, March 2012; Taj Mahal Review, June 2012; A World Rediscovered (An Anthology of Contemporary Verse), September 2012; Taj Mahal Review, December 2012; Harvests of New Millennium, January 2013; eFiction India, April 2013; eFiction India, June 2013; Taj Mahal Review, June 2013; eFiction India, July 2013; eFiction India, August 2013, eFiction India, October 2013, The Indian Trumpet (November-December 2013) and eFiction India, November 2013.

Surbhi Thukral

From This Moment Forth

Silvery moonlight bedecks their faces
As they dance to the sound of
Wind caressing the trees;
His hand about her neck
Like a string of dazzling gems;
Her cherubic smile brings upon his face
The radiance of all the stars in the night;
Intoxication reflects in their eyes
— it is the aperitif of love, certainly;
A promise of togetherness for all eternity
They make in the silent language of embrace,
Letting the rest of the world evanesce
From this moment forth
Than the two of them loving each other.

My Lover's Culpability

The heavy weight of time lost when
Beloved was in a foreign land
Melted in my eyes tonight.
Words unspoken for long
Poured as a melody of love.
He laid his hand on mine;
A shimmer of gold dazzled my eyes.
Felicity swerved to melancholy
By his broken vow of fidelity;
I swallowed splinters of broken trust.
"She was an obsession mistaken for love.
Your forgiveness I implore."
His voice filled with misery;
Eyes aglow with unabashed hope.
All hesitation fled as I bethought
Myself of the solitude endured.
"We are marionettes in the hands of fate."
My voice soaked in self deprecating compassion
Dusted off my lover's culpability

Surbhi Thukral

Forlorn Woman

Her heart is crushed;
Her sobs long and heavy
Upon hearing the death knell of her lover;
She is now like the restless waves of an ocean
Lamenting for the stars mounted up so high
Refusing to believe they cannot ever unite.
She runs to her domicile;
A reflection startles her eyes;
Another forlorn woman
Mourning the loss of her lover;
'We are the victims of fate, sister,'
She speaks in a consoling voice,
Pats the mottled mirror.

My Fate

Today, a ray of sunshine caresses my eyes.
A touch of moonlight arouses a passion inside.
A red garb shimmers behind a window display,
Pleading to me to hold on to faith.
A whirlpool of emotions ensnares me again
For a wonderland is promised again.
Oh! How can I ever forget?
When the trees were brazenly naked;
The winds had mercilessly rapped
On the islands of tranquillity;
When I was burned by the scorching sun;
Frozen as the day melted into the night;
When the happiness of the bridal feast
Was swerved to melancholy
By the sting of infidelity,
And I stood naked in the scrutiny
Of disdainful eyes — as if I were to blame;
When had fallen down the mountain of trust,
Crumbled between his hands
That once clasped mine in love.
Today, a drop of rain dares
To mollify such pain.
But, why protest?
May be, this time
Wouldn't be the same.
May be, someone, somewhere
Ameliorates my fate.

A Promise

A tint of golden light glistened in her eyes;
Let that fade as the pages of an aged book.
Her aura, the magical kiss of sunshine on a frosty day;
Let the days forever be darker than the nights.
Her words rescued the paralyzed hope of life;
Let them now wander as an orphaned child.
She blossomed out the deepest within me;
Let she be known as a lovely dream.
They say I am heartless;
She never said anything like this.
I look up to the azure sky;
It makes me believe, she never will,
For a moment before she'd slept
In its blue velvety arms
She took a promise from me

Shweta Kesari

Shweta kesari is a 2nd year engineering student.She is an avid reader and loves to spend time with books.She found immense pleasure in writing after reading so many books.For her,the best way to share her feelings and emotions is to pen down whatever strikes her heart.She has keen interest in music and stories.

Shweta Kesari

Silver Bullet

Tell those treacherous birds flying over sky
Make my existence felt by mighty moon
Oh dear pigeon! Ignite your wings
And lessen the distance between us
Tell the fiery not to boast his ability
Though my feet is on ground
My shadow is embossing over sky
Though I have never seen the first ray of sun
But it was me, who waited for you in its shimmering
shine
Tell those twinkling stars
Don't try to flatter my moon
In the night's gloom
Don't hide it in your tender cloudy blanket
The day when I will turn into star
I will grab away the radiance of the smoldering moon
Sojourning it in my heart

Few Words For You

In the cavern of my heart you lay
Hold my hand when the whether turns grey
My love for you is multiplying each day
Game of love and life, silently we play
Our meeting never bends to delay
When the morning wakes me with a sun's ray
Your face comes to my way
Hand in hand together we stray
A promise, has to be defray
My so called heart is flay
Our relationship never ends with fray
That's all I want to convey
No more words to say

Shweta Kesari

Lifeline

Flowers on my bed
Why I turned so red?
Should I go dread?
Amazed me, misled me
Is this injurious to health
Or a life beyond death
Half a loaf is better than no bread
Yet best thing since sliced bread
Though rush in where others fear to tread
Something nasty in the woodshed
Is this price on my head?
How I got embedded
In his glorious arms' shed
Should it go unsaid?
Or remain unread
Turned into a gad
Found on a mountain sled
Oh no! I am not sad
I am so glad
For life that's on my edge
It's just a mere pledge

Freedom

Where to hide, nowhere to go
Lovers eyeing me for the sake of their love
Heart screams no one to listen
Is there no heaven?
Or only I am locked up in hell?
Die or cry?
Why I am shy?
Just to loose yon faint memories
My love, my hate
Painful heart is my fate
Fellows stop me, but my heart is free
The only truth of my life
A bitter truth eaten by me
Washed me inside-outside
Pouring those loosely bound relation
Which has been shattered, it seems
Is it me?
Is it me?
Locked up but still free

Shweta Kesari

Some Lost Days

Though the meadow of my life has been lost
But those spring days has been captured
Captured in the celestial light
Yon rainbows will never appear again
Gone with all yon deity colours
An 180 degree turn it took
Tossing and turning my life on the bed of luck
The joy once I felt, I cannot feel anymore

Anjali Khurana

Anjali Khurana is a published author with Penguin Books India Pvt. Ltd in their latest anthology called Love Stories That Touched My Heart as a co-author. She comes from a place called Faridkot which is close to the Indo Pak border in Punjab. She speaks fluent Punjabi and loves to explore Sufism online. At present, she works with a media firm in Mumbai. Her core responsibilities include celebrity marketing, content acquisition, syndication & digitization along with ghost writing TV serials in her free time. She also manages Mumbai Freecycle ™, a nonprofit movement aimed at encouraging the art of giving to strangers.

Anjali Khurana

This Too Shall Pass

Quantum of happiness and tons of sorrow,
From you dear friend, some joy can I borrow?

Have missed by a whisker being with you,
And I'm in a state of denial this is true.

Life has shattered like a piece of glass,
It's a matter of time, this too shall pass.

My introduction once had your mention,
What may I do now, do you've a suggestion?

Will you forgive me if I were wrong?
Or ask for mercy and come along.

In an attempt to walk away from me,
You didn't realize, you walked over me.

Unrest in heart, my mind observes violence,
Can you dear friend, bring my world to silence?

I'll be indebted, if you extended your hand,
Please pull me out of this sinking sand.

For one last time, please hold me,
Look at me or love me or scold me.

I think of the times when you and I were 'us'
But you've stabbed my back, just like Brutus.

Please don't think I'm begging for affection,
Between us anymore, there's no connection.

But I have the will to ask a simple question,
What happened to our love and obsession?

Think of the times when we were together,
Trust me I believed they were forever.

I know this is a one sided conversation,
What else can I do to keep away depression?

My expression of love won't touch you alas,
It's a matter of time, this too shall pass.

Anjali Khurana

<u>Devoid</u>

It's not love that I'm devoid of ..
I'm devoid of you.
You may think that I've lost it ..
But this is true.
I'm devoid of you.

If I were good at expressing,
Life wouldn't be so depressing.
Without you, its black & blue,
I'm devoid of you.

I never made an effort or two,
To impress, to amaze, to woo you.
You never belonged to me,
But I'm devoid of you.

For you, I can go against the tide,
Without you, life's one hell of a ride.
I would never let you go
Coz I'm devoid of you.

<u>Old</u>

I have been told,
That I am too old ..
To have a crush,
To feel the mush ..
And to expect,
And then regret ..
Sob over thinking what's right & wrong,
And end up writing one more song…!!!

Well that's fine..
I wouldn't whine.
I'm ageing gracefully,
like an old wine.
Don't taste me in a haste,
Don't gulp me at once.
When you guzzle in your woes, take me along,
And then let me write one more song…!!!

If love is for young, what's for old?
Will my story remain untold?
I'm a couple of years bolder not older than you,
Can keep you in my heart of hearts,
You'd never be paroled.
With every passing season, I will write another
song…!!

Anjali Khurana

I must stop thinking over what's right & wrong,
And end up writing one more song..!!!